A COOL GiRL'S

Guide to

COURAGE

FIERCE QUOTES AND JOURNAL PROMPTS FOR FACING YOUR FEARS AND FINDING YOUR CONFIDENCE

CANDACE DOBY

sourcebooks fire

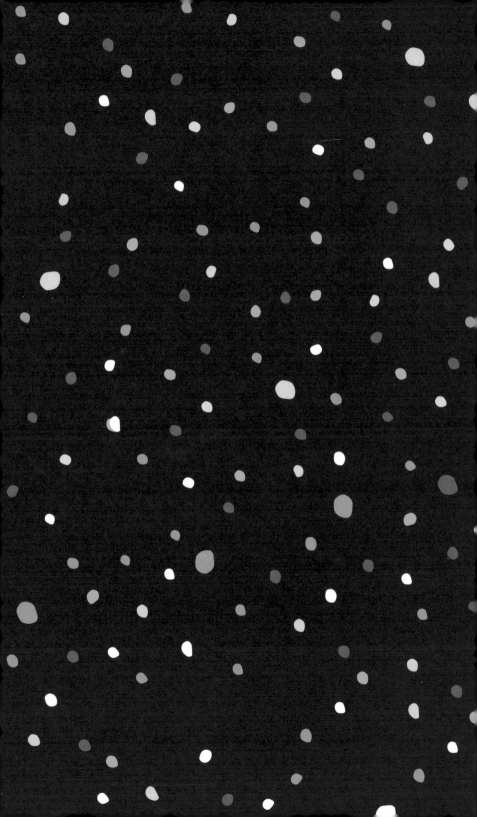

Copyright © 2020, 2022 by Candace Doby
Cover and internal design © 2022 by Sourcebooks
Internal illustrations by Annie Trudeau

Published by Sourcebooks Fire, an imprint of Sourcebooks
P.O. Box 4410, Naperville, Illinois 60567-4410
(630) 961-3900
sourcebooks.com

Originally published as *If Courage Could Talk* in 2020 in the
United States of America by Pep Talker. Original cover and
internal design by Annie Trudeau.

Printed and bound in China.
PP 10 9 8 7 6 5 4 3 2 1

Thanks, Mom and Dad,
for helping to build
courage in me.

CONTENTS

Do you, boo.   **5**

What's wrong?

You Scared?   **63**

Well...

Don't front. Confront.   **141**

Because

You are worth the risk.   **195**

DO YOU KNOW WHAT THE WORLD NEEDS, GIRL?

To see you shine.

Yep, the world is waiting for you to do your thing—to ignite your potential, step into your talents, speak like you mean it, and show your whole, real self in every space you occupy. But let's be honest: Fear has had a history of sassing you into a corner with its chest puffed out, double-dog daring you to pursue your wildest dreams.

All of the hype may have scared you into submission (and probably still does), but guess what? This is your time to take a chance...starting with listening to your courage. It's the candid inner voice that blends truth, love, and a little bit of shade to make you consider what's keeping you confined to the mindsets that block your greatness. The good news is you'll be introduced to this voice in the following pages.

This quote journal was created to be your side-kick to help you check your fears and do you, boo—to twerk to the beat of your own drum, no matter how offbeat you may be. Let it help you uncover creative ways to confront those pesky challenges threatening to keep you stuck and remind you that you are worthy of the goals you want to pursue.

There aren't set rules for how you should explore the journal. You can pick a random page to start from or a specific chapter that meets you where you are. Navigating through the book in sequential order, though, may help you to see how some quotes and prompts are connected. Whichever way you go, remember to digest the quotes like advice from a straight-talking friend who's on your team. And dive into the prompts with openness, curiosity, and recognition of how dope you are.

Did you pick up this book but aren't a girl? It's all good. This journal is packed with goodness that anyone with any pronoun at any age can find value in.

Before you jump in, write down the answer to this: What's one thing you really want to do that seems extra scary and too big to pursue? (Keep your answer in mind each time you flip the page.)

Do you, boo.

WHY aRE YOU

SLEE

☐ Last I checked,
☑ your goals
☐ weren't going
☐ to achieve
☐ themselves.

You've got bridges to CROSS

and boundaries to burn, baby.

You've got
TRUTH to
chase
and

dragons to Slay.

What's stopping you from confronting your fears and chasing your dream? Write down three specific obstacles that are blocking your shine.

ARe you waiting for permission?

Homegirl
is always
late.

Don't tell me you're
trying to Reach peRfection.

She neveR picks up.

ARe you looking FoR Validation?

That dude doesn't come outside.

Did you say you were avoiding failure?

He stays around the action.

F.A.I.L.U.R.E.

is just

another word

for

T.R.Y.

A.G.A.I.N.

B.O.O.

Failure isn't always fun. But, it doesn't seem so bad when you *reframe* it as an opportunity to try again. Describe other ways you can flip the script on your fears.

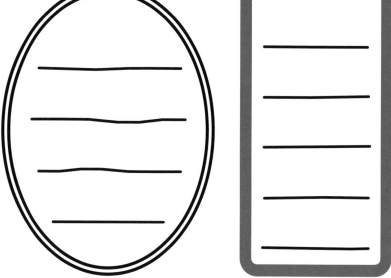

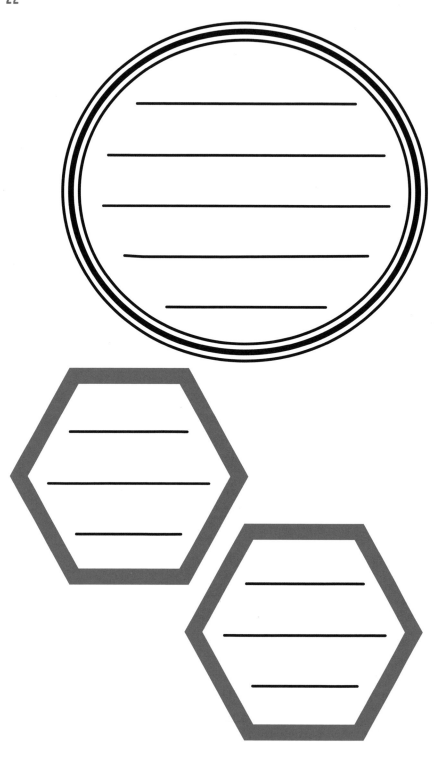

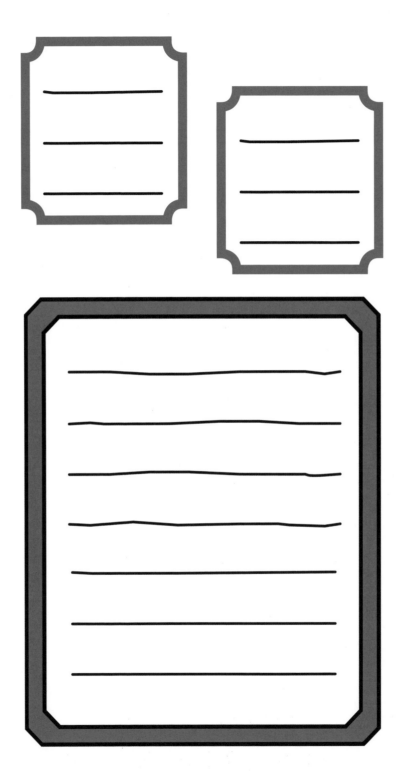

now that you've mastered

HOW

taking a

IF not
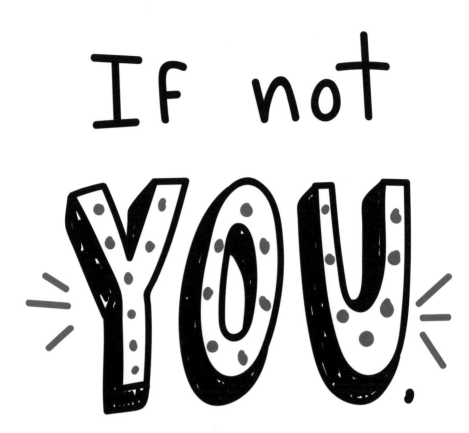
YOU,
then who...
CaReS?

What is one opportunity floating in front of you right now that you need to reach out and snatch? Describe it in detail.

_____

_____

_____

_____

_____

_____

_____

_____

_____

_____

_____

Unless you're posing for the paparazzi,

you should not
be standing still.

It's time

to put in

WERK

WERK

Something is wRong
when being stuck
in tRaffic botheRs
you moRe than being
stuck in life.

Reflect on your last big win. What was it and what did it reveal to you about yourself?

_____

_____

_____

_____

_____

_____

_____

_____

_____

_____

_____

_____

Self-doubt.

Drop it like

like

If self-doubt was a dance, describe fully how you would shake it off. (Don't be shy to get low.)

_____

_____

_____

_____

_____

_____

_____

_____

_____

_____

_____

_____

TRY lighting a FIRE uNdeR that booty.

Have you boxed yourself into a safe yet restrictive space (also known as your comfort zone)? List out five ways your comfort zone is cramping your style.

1 _____

_____

_____

_____

_____

2 _____

_____

_____

_____

_____

3

4

5

Boxes were made for takeout and donations to Goodwill — not you.

Since when are you ok
with being hemmed up
in a corner?

Move, chick-

Get OUT YOUR Way.

BURST YOUR

Define what "doing you" means to you. Write down three actions that would get you closer to doing your thing.

1

_____

_____

_____

_____

_____

_____

_____

_____

_____

_____

2

_____

_____

_____

_____

3

_____

_____

_____

_____

_____

_____

_____

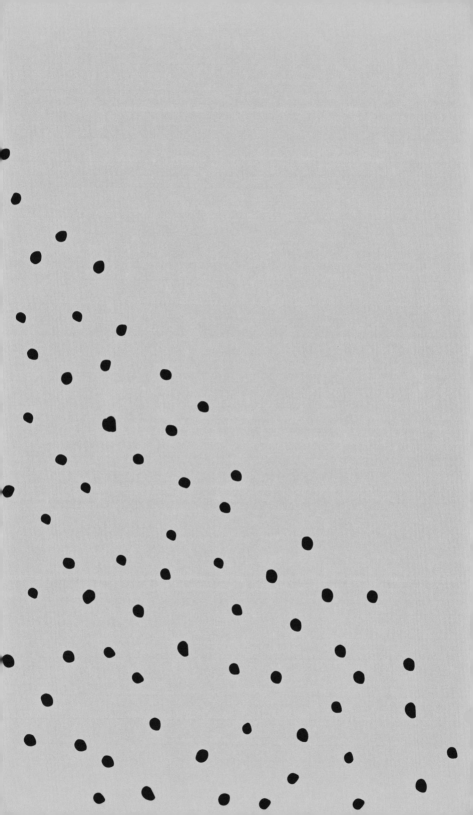

You
scared?

You Really gonna let fear talk to you like

Let's hear it: What does fear say to you to stop you from moving forward? Write down the phrases fear whispers in your ear.

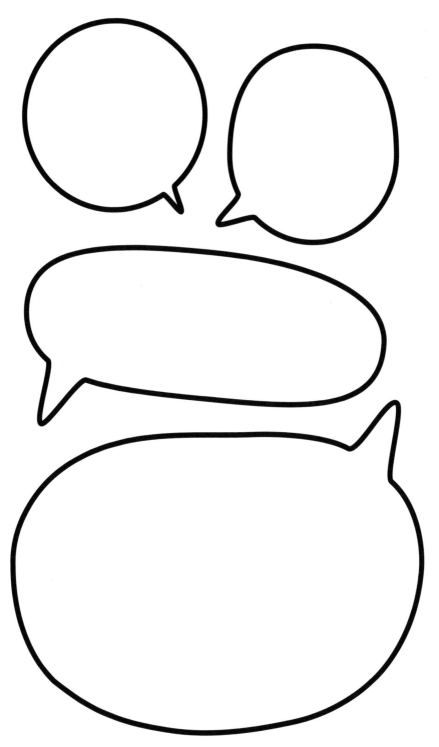

Of all the things you could fear, you're scared of being yourself?

What price
is fear paying
you to sell out
on yourself?

What's your worth? How do you determine your own value?

_____

_____

_____

_____

_____

_____

_____

_____

_____

_____

_____

_____

FINAL NOTICE

Are you going broke because fear is banking on your ignorance?

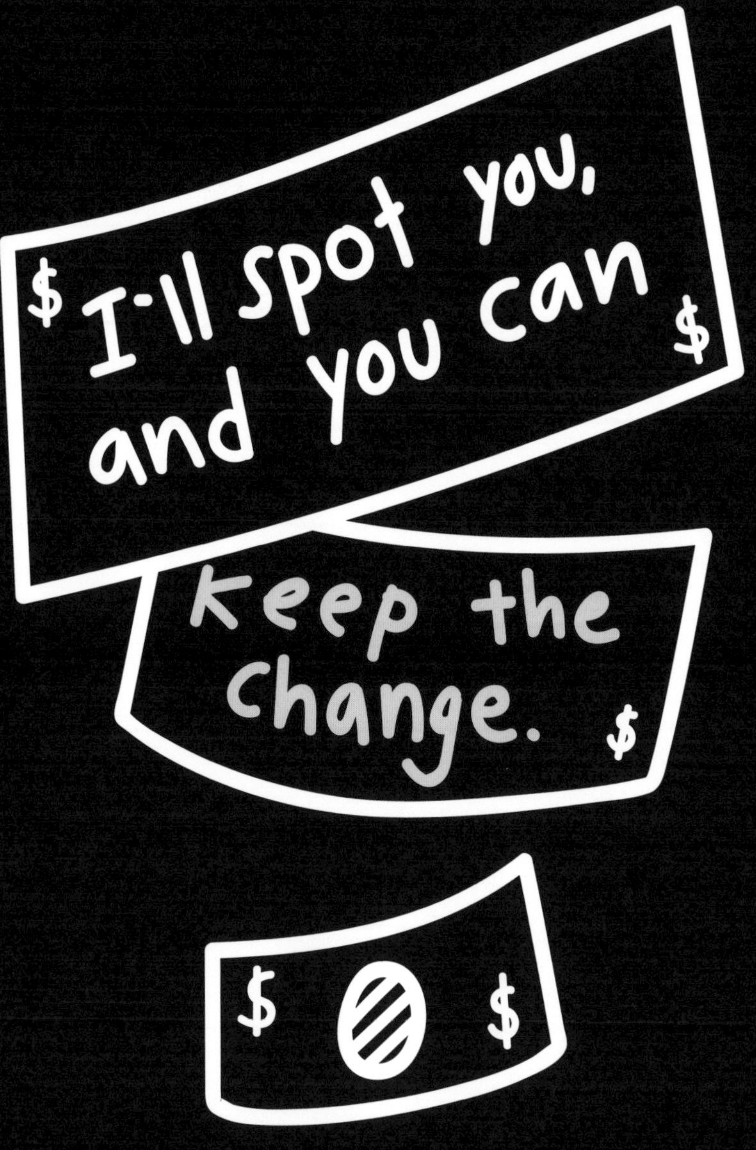
I'll spot you,
and you can
keep the
change.

Do you embrace change in your own life, or do you avoid it like a public bathroom?

_____

_____

_____

_____

_____

_____

_____

_____

_____

_____

_____

_____

_____

It's haRd
to secuRe the
bag

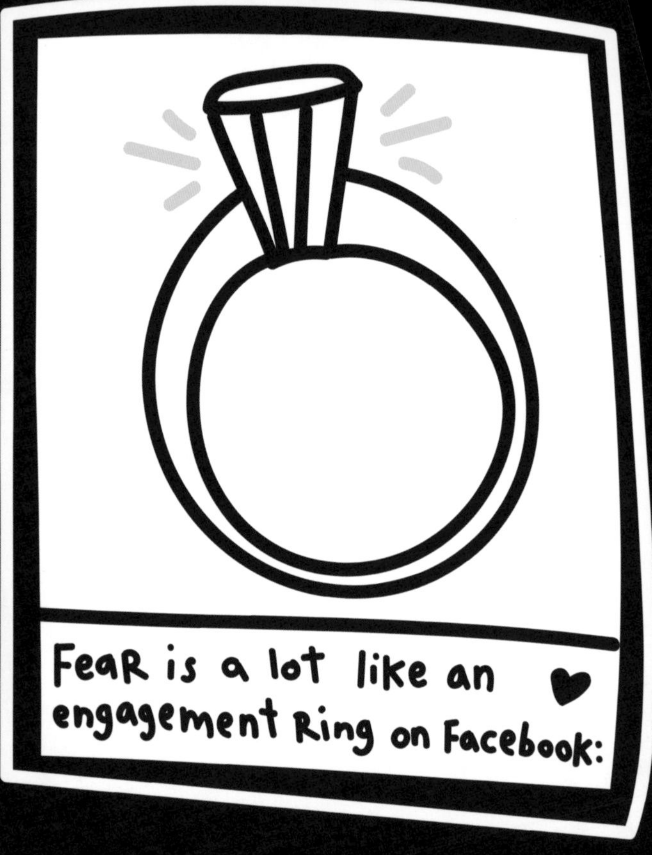

It looks bigger than it actually is.

Fear is like a
guy wearing a
pinkie ring: It can't
always be trusted.

On a scale of 1 to 10, how much do you trust your fear? Why?

1　2　3　4　5　6　7　8　9　10

_____

_____

_____

_____

_____

_____

_____

_____

_____

_____

FeaR is a caution.

So please
stop treating
it like a
conclusion.

If fear was a student, it would major in your problems - not your possibilities.

Picture a traffic signal. When your fear rises up, do you treat it like a yellow light and take caution or like a red light and stop? Why?

_____

_____

_____

_____

_____

_____

_____

_____

_____

_____

_____

I thought
you didn't have
time for games.

So, why are you letting fear play you?

You can't play to win

when
you're
always

on pause.

If going after your goal was a game, describe in detail the kind of player you would want to be.

_____

_____

_____

_____

_____

_____

_____

_____

_____

_____

_____

_____

_____

_____

If fear had balls, they would be in your court.

YOU'RE
SO
SCARED
OF
what
might
happen
that
YOU
ignore

What might happen.

You might not be a fortune-teller, but you can still imagine the possibilities of what could happen if you achieved your goal. Draw a picture of what life might look like when you reach your aim.

Keep dreaming. What else do you see?

Pick your battle:

Wax on, wax off. What mantras could you repeat to yourself to help you side-eye fear and stay focused on your goal?

_____

_____

_____

_____

_____

_____

_____

_____

_____

_____

_____

Settling isn't so bad When

you're settling into discomfort.

@courage

Clapback on your setback. #yas

Think about a time you went for something and missed the mark. Describe how you rebounded.

_____

_____

_____

_____

_____

_____

_____

_____

_____

_____

_____

_____

I know you like
being generous,
but please

stop
giving away
your power.

$\sqrt{you}$ F(E)A^R

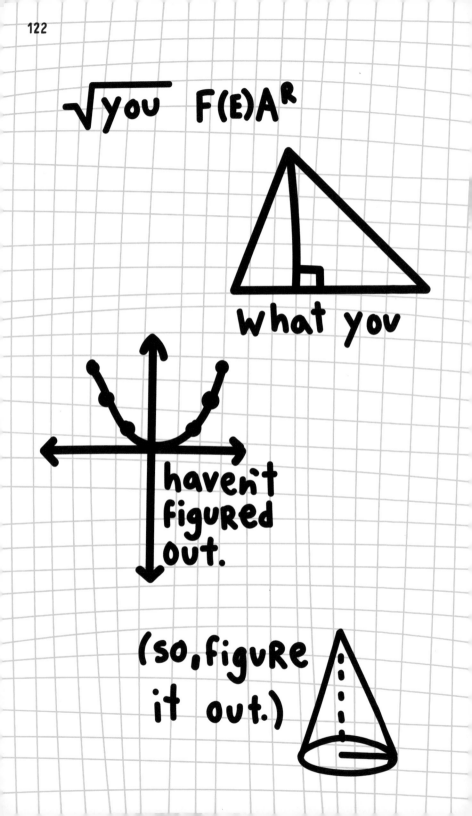

what you

haven't
figured
out.

(so, figure
it out.)

Be honest. Do you want to live life from your mama's couch?

☐ yes ☐ no

_____

_____

_____

_____

_____

_____

_____

_____

_____

_____

FeaR feeds off information.

Be a snack for
Instagram, not fear.

If you could serve up a snack to your fear, what would you feed it? List ten options. (And don't be scared to get creative.)

Question
your fear

like you question
your confidence.

Why are you afraid

of the shadow that's showing you how big you aRe?

If you were asked to offer up advice to your bestie to help them put their fear in check and get moving toward their goal, what advice would you give?

_____

_____

_____

_____

_____

_____

_____

_____

_____

_____

_____

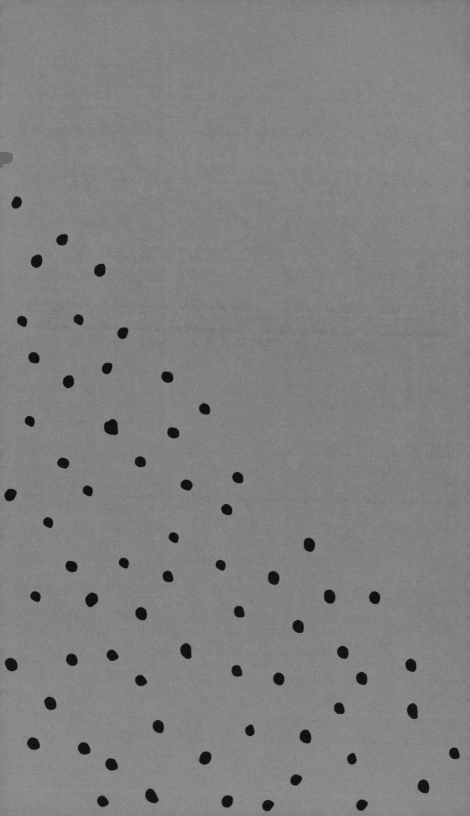

Don't front. Confront.

Confront your fear
like you confront

You might have forgotten, but you've got strengths. List five specific strengths you have that can help you go after your goal.

1 _____

_____

_____

2 _____

_____

_____

3 _____

_____

4 _____
_____
_____
_____
_____

5 _____
_____
_____
_____
_____
_____
_____
_____

You can't ignore
fear like you
ignore Robocalls.

Dodge
balls-

not fear.

You want a promotion?

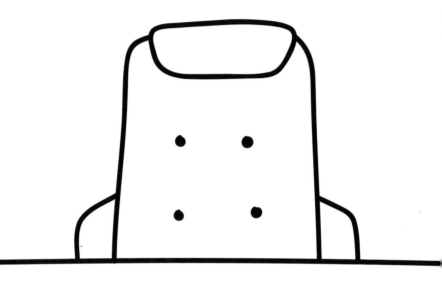

How about:

"Manager of Your Fear".

Talking to
your fear
isn't as weird
as talking
to your
TV—

At least
your fear
can hear you.

If you could have a conversation with your fear, what exactly would you say? Say it now (and throw all the shade you want).

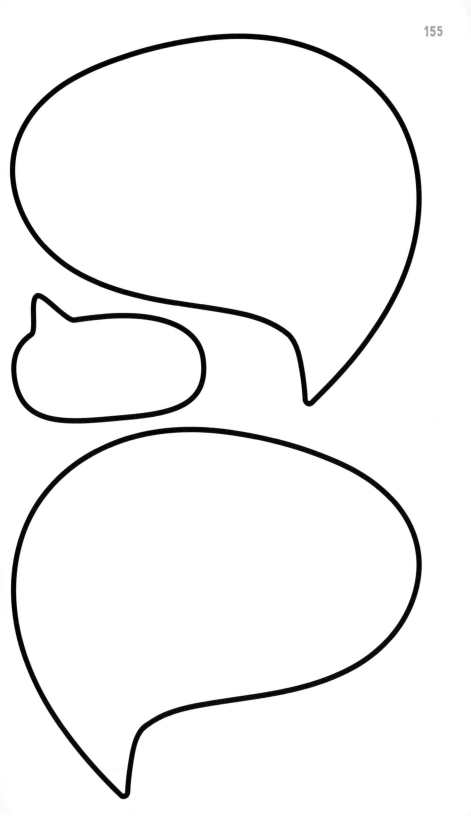

= #Relationshipgoals

Confronting fear is not the time to have commitment issues.

Fear falls back when you ANTE UP.

ARe your purpose
and values as
synced up

as Beyoncé's
Coachella
dancers?

Pause. What matters most to you about how you live your life? Do you know what your values are? Spell out your top five here.

1

_____

_____

_____

_____

_____

_____

_____

_____

_____

_____

2

_____

_____

_____

_____

3

_____

_____

_____

_____

_____

_____

_____

4

_____
_____
_____
_____

5

_____
_____
_____
_____
_____
_____
_____

Are your skills as tight as your skinny jeans?

Make a list of the skills you need to put your mission in motion. Which of them do you need to level up?

_____

_____

_____

_____

_____

_____

_____

_____

_____

_____

_____

_____

Is your confidence as high as your topknot?

What's an example of something you feel confident doing? Write out the steps you took to develop the confidence to do it. (Rinse and repeat the same process for your current goals.)

_____

_____

_____

_____

_____

_____

_____

_____

_____

_____

_____

Do you know yourself as well as you know the lyrics to The Golden Girls' theme song?

Just for fun, write out the lyrics to *The Golden Girls'*
theme song. You know you know them. (That's how
well you need to know yourself.)

_____

_____

_____

_____

_____

_____

_____

_____

_____

_____

_____

In oRdeR to do you,

you have to Know you.

If you want
to live out
loud, use your
inside voice.

Don't let conformity
con you out of your form.

Name three small baby steps you can take outside your comfort zone today in the direction of your goal.

1 _____

_____

_____

_____

_____

_____

_____

_____

_____

_____

_____

_____

2 _____

_____

_____

_____

_____

_____

_____

3 _____

_____

_____

_____

_____

_____

Don't
Stop.

Get it.
Get it.

There's no sense in

looking back unless

you're twerking.

Lace up your Chuck Taylors, and get to steppin.

You can't conquer what you can't confront. What are five things you could do to make your confrontation with fear less scary?

1 _____

_____

_____

_____

_____

2 _____

_____

_____

_____

_____

3 _____

_____

_____

_____

4 _____

_____

_____

5 _____

_____

_____

_____

_____

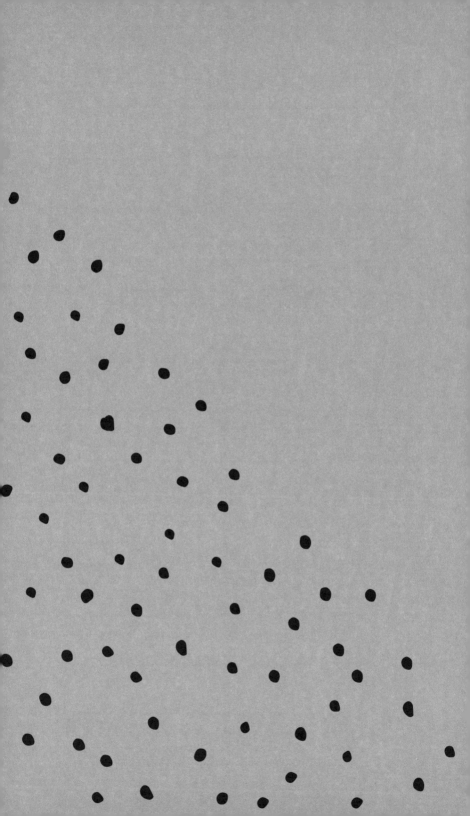

You are worth the risk.

Recognize

DOPE

YOUR

NESS

Flip your hair and brush your shoulder off. Then write down the reasons why you are worthy of having the thing you want to pursue.

_____

_____

_____

_____

_____

_____

_____

_____

_____

_____

_____

If you can bet on
a bracket, you can

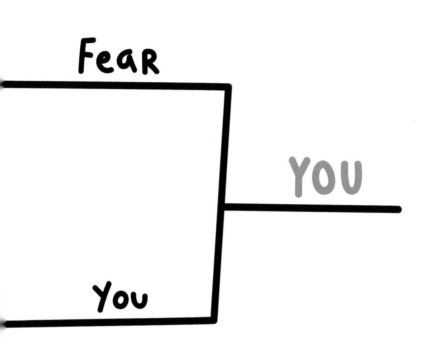

bet on yourself.

your comfort zone will be there when you come back.

YOUR

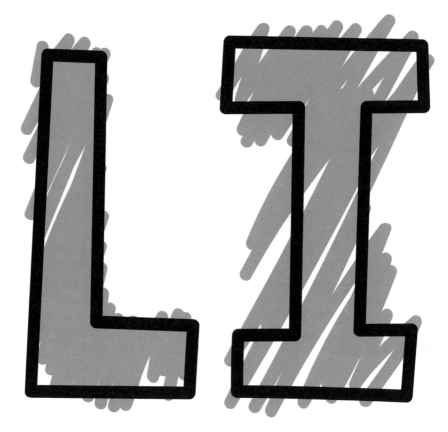

is not a coloring book -
you can go outside the lines.

Don't you want to know what you can become?

Describe the super-awesome person you hope to become in five years. What would you have accomplished?

_____

_____

_____

_____

_____

_____

_____

_____

_____

_____

_____

The only way to
find out is to

FIND OUT.

You can't collect the Reward without taking the Risk.

What are the three biggest risks of going after your goal? What are the three biggest risks of not going for it? Which risk stands out the most?

1 _____

_____

_____

2 _____

_____

_____

_____

3 _____

_____

_____

1 _____

_____

_____

_____

2 _____

_____

_____

_____

3 _____

_____

_____

_____

more than you trust TMZ.

If the chicken
can cross the ROAD,

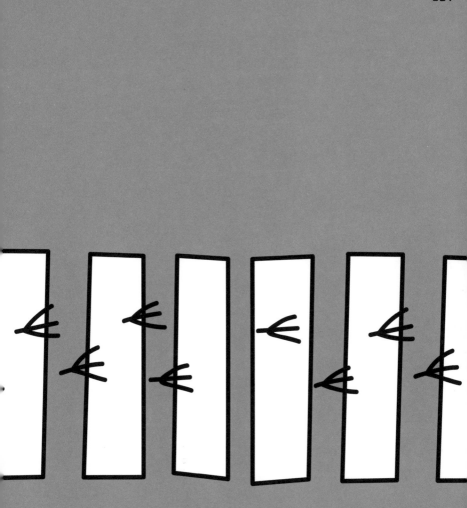

So can you, homie.

Hello from the other side.

Didn't you hear Adele?

Stop following
rules that
don't exist.

What are some of the make-believe rules you are following that make moving toward your goal harder than it has to be? (Hint: these are rules that only exist in your head.) What can you do today to break those rules?

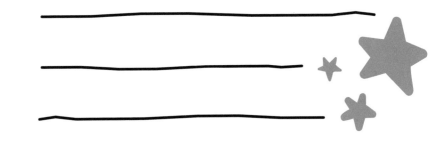

It's "start small and go slow".

Leap
OR get
dRagged.

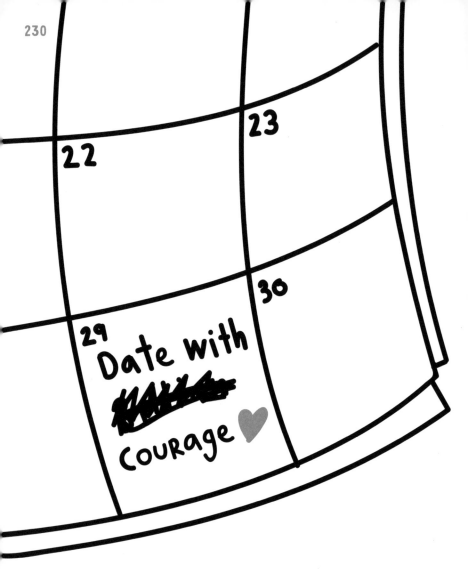

Stunt on your fear like you stunt on your ex.

Pretend like you're getting ready for a first date. What steps would you go through to get ready? How can you translate that process into getting ready to meet your fear?

_____

_____

_____

_____

_____

_____

_____

_____

_____

_____

_____

_____

_____

_____

_____

_____

_____

_____

_____

_____

_____

_____

_____

_____

_____

Don't
give up on
yourself
before you
take off.

Make a personal connection with your inner courage by drawing a character sketch and giving your courage a name.

"It's time to Ride out."

ABOUT THE AUTHOR

Candace Doby is a speaker, author, and coach whose mission is to make courage fun to talk about, easy to digest, and practical to activate. She works with universities and organizations across the U.S. to help young leaders build courage in themselves. She has spent a decade researching courage and combines that research with her experiences launching her own business, leading marketing teams at a global brand, and traveling the world solo. When she's not speaking or traveling, she's designing her line of Pep Talker greeting cards, sold online at pep-talker.com and in select stores. Candace is based in Atlanta, Georgia.

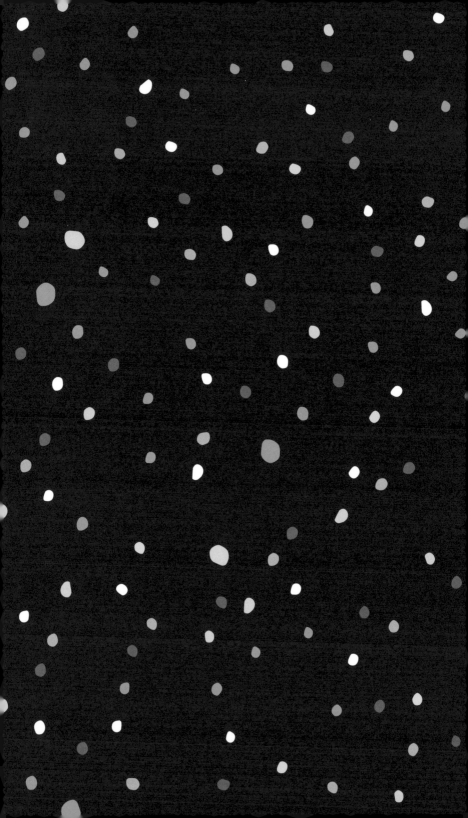

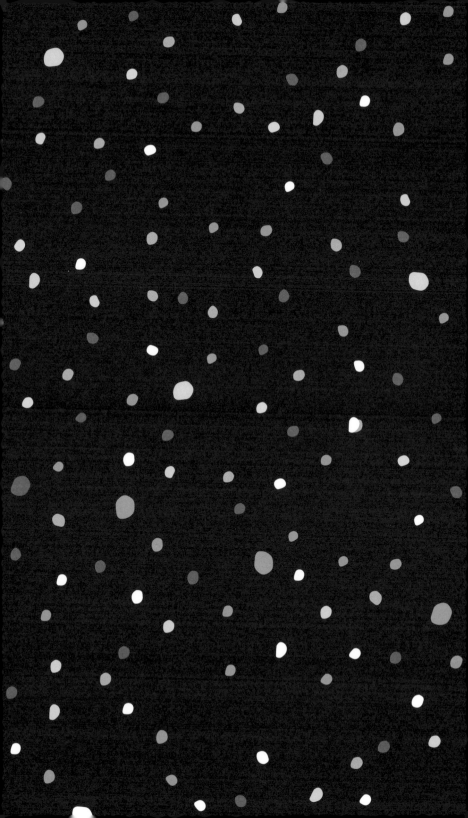